THE BEST NAME
OF SILENCE

POEMS BY
DAVID HELWIG

*To Bev, Don and Tom
for the great relief
of having you to talk to*

There is such innocence in this light.

The brightness presses on my skin
like the weight of fifteen feet of water.
The sailboats tack, come about,
slide over the waves.

The round bellies of women hang
like white brown golden tomatoes.
The braggart bodies of the swimmers
dive and splash and kick spray.

As the water reaches out for the horizon
it pulls up a handful of islands
and a white sail disappears
behind the green island trees.

Don't speak, don't say a word.

Pretend you don't know me
or the gods will grow jealous.

Four Seasons

*(The sun is a ball of hair
burning across all the distances.)*

1

The poplar holds yellow leaves
among green.

Rain darkens the air.

A clown sings tired old songs
and the leaves fall.

2

(After Prévert)

My fingers are motionless
on your skin.

Outside a train whistle blows.

Somewhere in the night
a horse is dying.

3

The wind cries out
in the empty trees.

I sit in a warm room, apprehensive,

think of Agamemnon
screwing Cassandra.

4

The snow is driven
on a horizontal slide

toward the end of time.

For quietness
rabbit tracks in the white.

5

We drove home lost,
drowned in the fog

then gone in a blur.

In the morning, pale light
covers your closed eyes.

6

A predominance of grey
on this spring afternoon,

the grass still dry and dead.

Here blossom only
pigs, pink in the warm sun.

7

The voluptuous sun licks your skin
and marks it. Dead fish

glitter like foil in the light.

You brush the sandwich crumbs
from your bare soft belly.

8

The first cold morning
breeds a restlessness.

Swallows chatter on a wire.

Leaves shake but the ragged bright zinnias
do not move on their stalks.

Poem in Acoustic Space

I am listening to time
moving through me, against me,
and to the singing
of your body in my hands.

Time is music on the skin
and the movement of my hands
finding the soft and smooth
and rough textures of you

is light in the mind.
You are continuous
as the universe
as I discover you

and I become the endless
light of where you are
and you are everywhere
through the time of time.

Beyond an open door
in the mixed light
of a bulb and an evening window
a woman stands naked
on a green towel
powdering herself
with scented powder.

She strikes the curve of her belly
and the powder explodes white
into the damp air and leaves
a patch of white on skin
that is brightened by hot water.

Beyond that open door
there is a woman
combing her dark hair
there is a woman
clean, perfumed,
with young breasts.
She stands on a green towel.

From beyond that open door
she walks toward me
a woman perfumed, naked
walking past me.

I do not touch her.

Landscapes

1

Across the room
I saw you in darkness
dancing your hair,
your dark hair,

later watched you
take off black
slacks, black boots,
black stockings;

saw your pale body

and darkness.

2

The bruise
has kept its pain
for a week.

I study it
every day
where it blossoms
red, green, yellow
on the white
splendid flesh.

The whiteness
is darkly marbled
with the trace
of damage and healing.

It looks like the map
of a new planet.

3

After two days
in the hot sun
you are burnt and sore
but white, white too,
where you were covered.

Your skin
is a patchwork
of red, white,
brown, white, red.

You are wearing a clown suit

a suit of pain.

4

Our bodies are galaxies,
each with a geometry
for its own space,

and the path followed
by any point
can be understood
only from inside
the space it moves in.

Or at the point
of intersection

where for a moment
your nipple rests
against my lips.

A Fragment from Sappho

Being a god, that's what it's like
to sit with you and listen from close by
to the way you talk, to hear you laugh.
My heart pounds in my ribs.

And when I look at you I stammer, can't speak,
my tongue is paralyzed, or I look
and a cold fire runs over my skin,
I sweat, can't see right or hear,
or I start to shake, turn pale,
sick, green as grass.
Sometimes I think I'm dying.

(And now I must learn to be content
with poverty, with separation.)

Melting

1

Now islands
are buckled to the world
on a shield of ice,

on a white earth and sky
the skaters, ice fishermen
are black hieroglyphs:

world's armourer, scribe
has encompassed

water, men, light.

2

You are far from here.
As the sun falls
it shines over the snow
and now I wonder
how your face looks
what you are wearing.

I have been reading
a book of love poems.

You gave it to me
how many years ago.

3

This cold Saturday morning
the sun shines down over
the stone fronts of old houses
making the surfaces look solid
as a limestone cliff face.

A man stands at an angle
by a closed door, looking down
the street, standing in sunlight
in a coat the colour of stone.

Along another street
a boy in a blue sweater
stands at a door
hunched against the cold
then walks inside.

4

When you are away
you are only memory
and absence.

And what shall I remember?

The recent early morning
when you left

or the red dress you wore
the first time I saw you?

The sky is torn between rain and snow.
The squirrels are moulting, their fur
ragged in the wet wind.

As the snow melts, the winter's
hoarding of dog shit appears
among the rotting leaves.

The grass is brown under the wind.

Your nipples shine
like dark soft pearls.

You open your legs
and the green world begins.

One-Sided Conversation

There are no pretty girls
                        I said

there are only

        those
by common agreement suitable
for magazines

        those
not much looked at

               and those
variously held sacred

or say you had a camera
there are those
you would never tire of photographing

which has nothing to do with faces
and something to do with

whatever you want

say a game of light.

Espionage Poems

I

THE BLOWN AGENT

I continue, of course,
living as I always have,
my habits unchanged.
I wear the same clothes
keep the same
expressions on my face.
There is no alternative.

I drink my coffee with cream,
do not smoke, behave as I ought,
shave with an electric razor,
continue all my commonplace behaviour.

There is no place to run,
my assignment was in a neutral country,
I am not likely in danger.
But I find it odd
to be what I pretended.

And each day as I turn the corner
of a familiar street, I feel
that I am watched from all sides
and everyone knows what I am.

2

THE CAMERA

Do not awake
for I am taking your picture
now, as you sleep.

It is a picture of your face
and as I take it
the lines of your face blur.

I have stolen them
for the secret room
where I have already
your feet and your breasts.

(Haven't you noticed
your sweaters no longer fit
and in the bath
you cannot see your toes?)

3

CRYPTOGRAPHER

Words are games.
I cannot read sentences.
I repeat pointless messages
in five ciphers
keyed to the bible.
I spend the night
creating palindromes
and word squares.
I have achieved
35 anagrams of your name.

(And once too
the world threatened
as sentences formed in my mouth,
words reached for response.

You had challenged me
to read with my tongue
the intricate calligraphy
of your skin.)

4

MATA HARI

She was temple dancer and whore, confessor
of a thousand men, the receptacle
of secrets upon secrets, a dancer
whose languid and marvellous body
destroyed the will of patriots,
the woman of secrets (Lilith perhaps,
the most inward of hidden women)
who would dance naked and sell herself,
was dangerous, accomplished and venereal.

Facing the firing squad, they say,
she opened her coat, showed the guns
her naked body and saved her life.

All this, lies of course.

She was a commonplace Dutch girl,
venal and selfish, had sagging breasts
and a plain face, sold herself where she could,
lied and mistreated her children.
She was executed
mostly as a political gesture.

All the same, one way or another,
she held the secrets of a thousand men.

And perhaps she dances now
in some limbo of lost armies
a perpetual sinuous dance
while the firing squad cover their eyes
and try to shoot.

Groundhog Day

I

When I got up from bed this morning
my head was thick with sleep
and I stumbled against the walls
as if I had a lame foot or had both feet
roped together. I moved down the stairs
awkwardly and rummaged through the house
for food. It took an hour of eating and walking around
to shake the sleep out of me. Awake
I went out into the day where it rained and rained.

All day long, snow melting, my feet
slopping through puddles of the first thaw,
the overcast hung about like sadness or more sleep.

The day stayed dark. At three o'clock
I looked at a window and saw my reflection
against the early dark.
              "Happy groundhog day."
I said those words to myself as I observed
the thickness of my furred body and the odd shape
given to my head by the rodent teeth.

On a day like this, I could be sure
the only shadows seen are the shadows cast
on darkness.

2

I'm a peace lovin' groundhog,
wish evil to none, just want to lie
in the clover in the sun
and eat and get me fat,
hole up for the winter
and as I nod to sleep recite
the wisdom of the fat:

when the cold comes
run away under the ground,
you got no dignity,
don't need none,

not in your hole in the ground.

3

We all have heard stories
of men without shadows
but who has heard
of the country where the shadows gather
who have lost men.
It is a land occupied
with erudite discussion of torture
with philosophy and hysteria.

There is a sound in the air
like electronic feedback.

Everything continues
in extension from shadow to shadow.

They talk and talk.

Somewhere away in an old cave
Brother Bear hugs his captive,
the girl who passed you once in spring
with daffodils in her hand.

She loses the days in his arms
awake, motionless, coupled with him
for the length of his winter
wondering what will come
when he wakes.

Will he set her free to walk
out of the cave? She lies blind
to all but the black fur
that covers her eyes,
lies hugged in the slow heat
of his sleep.
                        She remembers
how he came out of the woods
walking on two legs like a clown
as she turned from washing in the bright water
felt the sharp October air
and ran toward her clothes.

Now loses her days, open eyed, wondering.

Suddenly he snorts awake,
moves from her and walks abroad
seeking his shadow.
                        She goes
out of the cave and looks about her,
cold and lost.

5

"Groundhog, groundhog,
what makes your back so brown?"

"I been livin' in the ground
Too darn long.
Drown, drown,
It's a wonder I don't drown."

6

February 3

A freezing morning. The ruins of the thaw
powdered by a light snow. Three
grey squirrels sit in a grey tree.
Clarity is restored by the way

the sun shines on us. I sit alone
in a tidy room and drink clear tea.

Barn Poems

I

The window is a hole
in the flat
wall of the old
barn. A little light
shines in.

The barn is dark. Inside
the walls around the hole
are dark with age and dirt.

Looking outside, the eye
moves past branch behind branch
leaf behind leaf to the narrow
holes into the sky.

The eye moves outward
to the narrow vents
of sky, the sun
moves down between the ranks
of branches and the leaves
move in the wind changing
the shape of sky and
of sun.

Across the hole
hanging on a piece of web
drops a spider
eight-legged dancer
suspended
where the wall is not.

And there
where the wall is not
between the dark inside
and the ranks of leaves,
moves, extruding
the thin web that he spreads
across the hole where the eye
meets the light.

2

The wasps are blue
dark as black, iridescent,
trail their delicate legs
blue dark
as black metal
across the dark roof,
buzz over the brown
old pine boards,
hang in the hot air
of the barn windows.

They are all around me,
their armoured bodies
envenomed,
their hard blue shells
sail over my head,
disappear in the small holes
of mud nests,
crawl out and sail past
dangling their jointed legs.

And I sit quiet
in this house where wasps
surround me, buzzing
envenomed, blue
dark as black.

Wild Asters

They grow in prodigal purple
thousands by the roadsides
and in the fields, giving
away their fire, their
beauty and knowing nothing
of what they give, without pride
or the intentions of men,
only growing, only burning
prodigal, unproud clusters
of bright flowers everywhere
by the road.

Rock and bird
ocean and rock
the sword taken
the passage on
through peril
the fated way
of men at arms:

kings are throned
on the decorum
of their leave-taking.

My legs rise and fall
pushing, turning
the wheels of the bicycle
along the street.

Two black crows
sit on fence posts
beside the road.

Round berries
of the hawthorn
hold the light.

Morning and afternoon
my legs rise and fall
(the leaves making
their gradual bright
accumulation of death)
and into the evening
the bike wheels turn.

A fat orange moon
hangs in the darkness
as I ride past.

Toward Winter

This is goose summer, the time of spiders.
In the hectic wind and colour of the air
the spiders build their intricate webs and stand
waiting, their eight legs and two-part bodies
at the centre of the web's geometry,
an emblem of silence.

The apples are ripening now,
the sky taunts me with brightness.
The geese move in a close white group,
move white and fat with the smooth flow
of grain under the wind. Pure and sensual
is the fat gander love I feel for them
and for the women who walk in the cool sunlight
and for all things.

Now as the year approaches some fulfilment
of old prophecies, somewhere
the Spider King stands
on the viscid threads of his web
and waits for me to reach fulfilment
to be full and still.

I remember a day
when I sat beside the lake
and saw a distant point of land
suspended in air.
Behind me
in a building locked for the winter
a telephone rang and rang and rang.
A suicide case, I thought,
making one last call for help
to the wrong number.

For hours this morning
I was convinced that some disaster
had overtaken me in my sleep.

This is goose summer, strangeness takes us.
This is the time of the year
when spiders fly, leaping into the wind,
ballooning like kites at the end of their draglines,
sometimes found two hundred miles from land.
And now their webs are blown into the air
to fall as gossamer, our Lady's threads,
another gift of the sky and the Spider King.

But me, I walk the earth,
blunder into the sticky webs
that hang all around me.

Maybe something did happen in my sleep.
Maybe I met the Spider King
and had nothing to say.

That telephone call in the locked building—
maybe it was for me—someone
sending me word, demanding an account.

What can I say?

This: I wear the officious feathers of an old gander
going about my business, going about
my business under the far sky.
I await my metamorphosis, the day
when I will unriddle the emblems of silence

but I make fire wherever I look,
at the white geese, the grey barns, the sky.
Each blade of grass is a green flame,
the flowers are too hot and bright to touch.

I am an arsonist going in the disguise
of foolish alien feathers.

A Poem in February

(For Bev)

>Winter lilacs
>   a clustering
>of branches, twigs.

In the branches a flock of starlings,
one after another flying down
to search for food; one flies
away, another takes its place
in the bare twigs. One the same
as another, speckled, black.

The branches move in the wind
over the snow, under the grey
presence of the sky. The black
starlings come and go.

>Black bird,
>   awkward handful
>of dark feathers
>   like an old black
>rag in the cold.

When the birds are gone, flown away,
the lilacs remain, empty against
the wind, between snow and sky.

What fills the tree when the birds have gone?
What does the hand hold that holds nothing?

>The winter trees
>   construct an emptiness
>they do not fill.

The Last of the Proms

London, 13 September, 1969

Eight years ago in England
we watched with her,
our ancient stinking friend
who lived each day
in keen and hunch-backed concentration
on her television set,
and she explained to us
strangely, lovingly
(her mind jumbling past and present)
the ceremony of this concert,
how the young people
would sleep all night in the street
waiting for tickets
and would join in singing at the end.

She has been dead
a long time now,
gone hump-backed, stiff-legged
into the empty years,
not again to refuse to sit
by a "nigger" on a bus
nor to listen bright-eyed
to this music,

but I am here again
remembering her and that night,
and hundreds of the gay white young
are here singing "Rule Britannia"
and "Land of Hope and Glory"
as she loved to hear them sing
at the last of the proms.

The Blue Feather: Four Poems from England

1

My children are playing in a distant room.
My temper these days is bad, worse
than ever. Loneliness makes me angry
at interruptions.
    The Moslems
march in the street, and jets
come in to land over this house.

No-one would believe how many planes
are in the air.
    Hundreds of Moslems
march through the streets
chanting war. The English police
march alongside to keep order.

A child is coming closer. I calm myself.

Arab explosives, fire-bombs, appear
and strike this city.
    We flew
all night to get here.

2

The English train, domesticated, limited
in its speed and distances,
stopped a dozen times
in the endless city.

At first the track
was crowded with houses, factories.

The hazy summer
hung softly over the earth
and at last the view opened
on green fields, a benediction of rivers.

3

AT THE ZOO

The Punch-and-Judy show is caged
in years. Under the blowing clouds
of a fine English September day
the children cry out at the gay cruelty
of Mr. Punch. Who cracks the baby's head.
Who crows like rooster, strikes and kills
until the crocodile carries him away.

I sit far back. I can't hear all the words,
but my children come back to me enchanted,

and we move on to see the lions fed.

4

You have gone home. And I sit here
in the shabby living-room of our flat.
I think of lighting the gas fire,
not for heat, but for the company
and comfort of its burning.
      You have gone
and are home, preparing somehow,
preparing for your mother's funeral
in what I remember and imagine
as the impossible brightness and beauty
of the fall there, the sun now low,
toward setting, the air growing cold
and the jays screeching, flashing
their blue feathers across the yard
where your mother fed them.
      We had
a feather, blue, the feather of a jay,
given to the children to bring here
and keep, and child me, I loved it more
than they did and lost it somewhere,

have only the memory of that feather
and my mind's picture of you there
where the hills are so bright in the bright air
that they tear the eyes from the head.

I am here. In England. The children are sleeping.

("How small such things, domestic, *kitsch* almost,"
says Eli Mandell, and I ask him this:
if we are not to love our children now,
when shall we love them? Is it better
to love them only in the hands of the commissars
and gauleiters, or to see them now,
here asleep, and in this country
that is not their home?)
                            They sleep.
You have gone home.
                        Decently at best
the funeral will be made, for we have no prayers
but our silences, and the voices of the earth
will go on, daily, daily, in the woods
and in the fields.
                   The blue feather
is lost somewhere. I put it in a book
of poems, to keep, because I liked it,
but it is gone into poems and memory
as Canada now, an imagined place
of strict decencies and the vast air,
where love might have prospered, and where
(as Dennis Lee would have it) we have failed.

How can I know? I am here. I am not there.

Tomorrow the funeral will be observed,
death, earth, the act of death
lit by the brilliant air, an end
of moving, death, earth, air,
while here in England, I live the dull
tender impossibility of caring for our children.

At Kew and Beyond

A snowflake trembles at the edge of darkness.
The railway station is bare and cold.
I wait for the train to come toward me.
It will cross a bridge over the river.
The train rattles. Clouds are silent.
Snowflakes melt as they strike the water.
The river runs on toward the sky.
A man walks slowly in an empty street.

On the station platform by the long track
A man touches his wife's pale hair.
I see children playing in the snow.
A snowball flies through the air, strikes.
The boats in the Thames are quiet at their moorings.
The gulls move on their bent wings
Between the grey river and the grey clouds.
The train goes past them to the great city.

When the train leaves, the station will be empty.
The brick walls are dark from old smoke.
I wait as each morning I wait for letters
Here where I pass the winter in a strange city.
The train moves out over the dark river
Where the reflected lights glitter in silence.
I see a hundred windows, an empty park.
Darkness unites the river and the sky.

Hooker at Christmas

Photograph: an unknown woman
gives birth, her flesh torn wide
by the child's wet head.

In the yard, below an empty tree
green pears rot where they fell
in the damp grass.
                    Our soundest knowledge
is to know that we know him not
as indeed he is, neither can know him
and our safest eloquence is our silence.

Riding home in the evening dark
on the top of the London bus, we saw
the heads of two pigs in a butcher's window.

My daughter said the heads were smiling.
And they were.

Balearic Winter

      All afternoon, the wind
has come from the sea to beat on the white walls
 of the island. The trunk of the Balearic pines
are bent from its force, and all day long
  I've thought of Chopin wintering on Majorca,
setting on paper the dainty marvels of his brain
 while the delicate webbed grip of his lungs
on the precious air grew slack and shallow,
  and he coughed, tried not to breathe, listened to rain.

Outside this room, the wind is fast and loud
 against the windows and against the door
  that leads to our balcony. I sink in a chair
to work in the half-light and whistle between my
   teeth
 a Chopin nocturne.

      In the mornings here
the young *émigrés* from Europe and America
 sit outside a bar in the main square
or walk through the narrow white streets of the old
   city
  past doorways that lead to dark small rooms and
   windows
where caged birds sing. A boy and girl will sit
 in shelter against a wall, eating an orange.

Beside the road, daisies with yellow centres
 and single scarlet poppies are growing wild
among the almond trees, and by a white house
  the orange trees are thick and bright with fruit.

In the afternoon, children walk on the beach
to gather shells, the miraculous common harvest
   of the shore, cowries, starfish and all
the delicate architecture that is made
   and dies in the body of the sea, that children,
wise and wilful, gather in the lust of beauty
   and carry away, carrying to closed rooms
the faint smell of the sea.

                                  Beside this sea
   shut up on Majorca, Chopin coughed in the rain
of the Balearic winter, an *émigré* writing down
   melodic effete nocturnes and songs in praise
of Poland where he did not live. While Sand
   comforted him and smoked and brooded and
      worked.

Late in the afternoon, the sun, bright as a poppy,
drops westward to the Atlantic, always westward,
   like the gold that tempted west the burning eyes
of the conquistadors. Falling always, the sun
   drops into the ocean, under the Atlantic
to the golden sensual underwater cities
   that hang on the branches of the sea like oranges.

As the white walls darken and the island loses its
      gold,
   the *émigrés* smoke drugs in tiny rooms.
I drink white wine and coffee, and I think
   of those dainty effeminate fingers playing
      nocturnes
through all the wind and rain and fear of death
   of that Majorcan winter.

Ibiza, February 1970

I saw her standing there
in a country of flowers,
my daughter, standing
with flowers in her hands,
the yellow daisies and pale yellow
daisies, and a single ragged
scarlet poppy, standing there
lost in the field, the yellow
of a thousand flowers, her sweater
as red as a poppy, beneath
the trees, beneath the hills
in the light of the noon sky,
in flowers, yellow flowers,
in a field of flowers, holding
yellow daisies and the one
red poppy in her hands.

A Walk Down Piccadilly

three
Japanese
snapping
pictures
of
one
Japanese
snapping
pictures
of
three
Japanese
snapping
pictures
of
one

Kew Gardens

The light is silver
on the wet leaves.
The ancient wind
ruffles the pond
around the statue
of Laocoon and the snake.

This is a garden, green,
composed, yet fallen leaves
are driven in the wind
like crowds running
in panic or rage.

The statue, man and serpent,
tangled in bronze.

This is a garden, the walls
keep it, the wind here
is shaped by the poised
trees and lawns it crosses.

Wind, garden,
man, serpent,
garden, serpent,
wind, man.

The light is silver.

Journey

Bird song over the city streets,
trees in blossom, and beside the train
daffodils, gardens, allotments,
willows in the Thames at Richmond.

(Far across the windy park, I saw
a girl in a short dress run
on long legs and awkward shoes
chasing her son's ball, the father,

as they walked out of the park, reached
his arm around her waist.) Tonight again
I'll sit by the bedside of a woman
who may or may not be losing

a three-months foetus. The doors of the train
clatter. The station is suddenly silent.

After the Deaths at Kent State

                    Today I see
gardeners in a formal garden
in a far country, here in England
surrounded by spring, by gentleness
and the smell of the green growth.

(A girl so thin I can see each muscle
move as she moves, walks
through the garden, writing in a book.)

In a shop, a man diseased appears to dance
behind me all round the shop. I hold the hand
of a child that is not my own and think
of the far-away dead, for them
there are no gardens.

Elegy

". . . later I found out that Julio Zenon Acosta had died on the hilltop. That uneducated and illiterate guajiro *who had understood the enormous tasks the Revolution would face after its victory, and who was learning the alphabet to prepare himself for this, would never finish that task"*—Che Guevara, Reminiscences of the Cuban Revolutionary War

Julio Zenon Acosta, did the Cuban bugs
pick your bones on that jungle hilltop
where you died twelve years ago?
Did the green snakes coil in your ribs?

In the days before that day
you walked through the dangerous hills
carrying supplies and the weight
of your gigantic hopes, one by one
adding the letters of the alphabet
to your kit. Dying too soon,
your death was a silence, a screaming
hole in the world on a Cuban hilltop.

Waiting on that hilltop
at 45 years old
a peasant who gave his love
to the words of strangers
was killed in a surprise attack.

A man had betrayed your comrades. They ran
into the green of the deeper forest,
left blankets, medical supplies
and left your body,
one letter in a nightmare language
written on a Cuban hill
where your hope of words ended.

Twelve years later, Julio Acosta,
I imagine your bleached bones
somewhere in Cuba and your body
part of the Cuban earth, and I bring
these letters of my foreign alphabet
to speak of your interrupted task
and your wordless death.

Prelude to Politics

Think of Agamemnon
screwing Cassandra

thrusting himself in while prophecy

poured over his head
like blood.

Cities

We name them often as a way of naming death,
the hard death of concrete, all the deaths that can
   be died
alone as men turn their heads, passing, and puzzle
   themselves
with what to think or say as the light of splendour
falls away from the flesh and death names itself on
   the lips
of the falling man. We name them for the crowd
of men that die there each day, as the pale yellow
haze hangs in the air like bad music and the cars
tear off the fingers of silence and the signs flash and
   quiver
like the involuntary shudders of a seizure,
the lights declare their colours like a man declaring
   his hatred.
We name them dead, dying, because we cannot
   think
of what we know, because there are so many souls
   we'll never have,
bodies we'll never love, and the cost of money
gets higher every day.

And the cities darken, the concrete hardens and
   narrows, a man walking
sees nothing but walls, and the child is soothed
by engines throbbing and suckled on the sour reek
   of the air
until his throat burns and reddens as he grows to
   find
that his feet are anchored in cement, that he can only
stand still and watch the grey walls hunt him down
until he would be glad of a coffin for space, of death
   for silence.

The cities darken. We name them death and
   go from drive-in to drive-in
locked in our cars. And down at the centre
the dark is darkest, the air has been stolen
and sold, and as we bend under the weight of
   buildings
and eat our money, we open our sore red eyes
and see at our feet in darkness a movement, a
   presence that is sudden
and mysterious, a bug presence, bug self, the
   dwarf soul
that we have harboured and ignored, and in a small
   hoarse voice
the bug self says "You, useless citizen, who voted
for ecstasy and then wondered what it meant,
citizen of longing, subtle policeman, you alderman
   of new clothes,
I register my approval of all you never did,
the killer you hesitated to worship, the regret at
   the edge
of action. Citizen of regret, passenger, the movies
   are free and sexy,
but once you ignored the screen and took the hand
of the sad giant beside you who wept with a soft
   sound
like the rustling of bedclothes. Once, friend, on
   the bus
in the early morning you looked in a window
   and saw
a man standing beside a table, once in a junkyard,
   the light
caught a discarded chrome bumper and made you
   blink.
Citizen of forever, there is a darkness between your
   toes where the amoeba
may begin once more his ascent into the murderous
   cities.
Citizen of regret, the city is a darkness on the face
of the deep and God has not yet commanded it
   to be."

Vision

This is the night when the anarchist dreams of
    heaven
and gives his dreams away by handfuls.

The Bolsheviks burn. Their eyes have turned to
    guns.

This is the night when the anarchist dreams of love.

The Bolsheviks burn like paper.

This is the night when the anarchist dreams of
    freedom,
his dream so rich and deep
that after he wakes, sweating and shaking,
he doesn't dare remember it.
And this is the night when the anarchist dreams of
    peace,
a place of silence where no-one is ravaged
by the travelling teeth of the hours.

This is the night when the Bolsheviks burn.

Someone is here. Open your doors.

Scene from a Movie

The old railway tracks run down the edge of the city
between the houses and the broad river. The water
is almost still early in the morning, and the trains
seldom use this track, and early in the morning
when the air is clear and the sky is high and light,
it is very quiet in these fields down by the river.

There is a man lying in these quiet fields
near the edge of the reeds, asleep, in a heavy coat,
the dew all over him and around him, asleep
in the early sunlight. I do not know his name,
but I see him there far out at the edge of town
where the sun rises and the breeze moves the water
with a touch as light as the touch of fingers.

There is an empty wine bottle shining at his side
and there is a girl, a young girl, she is fourteen
    years old,
coming down the hill in a summer dress, light blue,
almost the colour of the early sky
but flecked with grey as the sky today is not.
She walks down through the wet reeds, down
    toward the river.

The girl, as she turns to walk along the tracks,
sees the fallen sleeping body of the man in the grass,
and she walks toward him and stands on the cinders
    by the track,
looks down at the man. She walks down the slope
and into the grass, walking across to the sleeping
    man
and standing there in her blue dress looking down.
She bends down, and with quick delicate fingers,
unties his shoes and takes them off his feet.
She stands up. She has grown rapidly this year and
    is almost tall
as she walks away carrying the shoes.

She walks down a familiar path by the long reeds
to the place where a willow tree hangs over the river
and she stops there. She stands by the willow
in the early sunlight, and she throws the first shoe
high into the air. It turns and flies and falls
with a splash like a fish jumping. She lifts
the other shoe and throws it from her,
up, out and down. Splash. The shoes are gone.
And she turns and walks back up the familiar path
past the place where the man still lies sleeping,
his face asleep unworried and his feet without shoes.

(I do not know where I am in the picture. I think
I am not there, unless I am the man I see
vanishing over the top of the hill with a camera.)

Poem for the End of the Revolution

The revolution is over
and never began, though
Winstanley dug up the Commons
and Nechayev (Agent 2771
of the World Revolutionary
Alliance—which didn't exist)
killed the informer Ivanov
in the name of a future
that would not come
for we never knew
what time was, at least
not well enough.

(Alone on a moving bus
riding to Montreal,
the city of soldiers,
riding through a landscape
of rocks, rivers and the warm
colours of a dying year,
I thought of the hands
that closed the throat
of Pierre Laporte
and in the name of freedom.)

Marx said: "Time is
a locked spiral, and freedom
is knowing you were never free."

(As the bus drove into Cornwall,
the houses were so heavy
with the dust of life
that it seemed to me
I'd lived in every one.

And I found myself
looking at the windows,
the bare trees, grey sky,
here at the edge
of a strange town, remembering
what it was like
to be the child
of ordinary people
on an ordinary afternoon.)

And Tolstoy laboured
for a revolution too pure
to be touched by the hands of men.
He said: "Time is not real,
only love, only the Kingdom of God
is real. And I am getting old
and they will not give me peace."

(As we sat and talked
high over Montreal,
a woman's voice
from fifteen floors below
screamed wildly, angrily,
but all we could hear
were the letters FLQ.

My friend said
that if he spoke French
he would join
Le Parti Québecois,
but as it was
he only wanted a divorce,
a difficult matter
since his lawyer
was now in jail.)

The revolution goes round
and round. A dance,
the double dance
of politicians and killers,
dancing our history
into melodrama.

(The next day I arrived
in Fredericton where
there was no-one
I had ever loved.)

The question is, what
was the question we could
never quite remember?
It had something to do
with the past, the future;
we say history, we say
the revolution, we say
what is beyond our being
that will hold in itself
childhood and death, work
and what we've loved.

We, you, I, them,
is, will be, was.

The revolution never began
and is never over.

Words from Hell

*(For Brian Ensor, killed in Kingston Penitentiary
18 April, 1971)*

I was eighteen when I came in these gates
on a sentence of indeterminate duration.
I was eighteen and twisted, and your courts
sent me away from sexual temptation.

I could not keep my fingers off your children.
Your little girls set all my flesh on fire.
I did some things I knew you had forbidden.
You put me in a cell and closed the door.

My need was hideous to the violent men
around me, and they changed my face to mud,
my prisoned life to freedom in the land
of death. Coloured their weapons with my blood.

They beat the life from me with iron bars.
They beat me in a dance of joyous hate.
I cannot count the wounds my body bears.
I was eighteen when I came in these gates.

Considerations

Any country is only a way of failing,
and nationality is an accident of time,
like love.
          That I was born
in Toronto in an April snowstorm
makes nothing certain.
                       That I remember
ducks flying in the winter twilight
of Lake Ontario means only this,
that I was there, and I remember it.

Still, to have a country is to have
a way to encounter history in the streets
of a burning city whose fire is our own.

That we have less killing, more absurdities,
some luck, a bit of time,
and memories like those winter ducks
is about as much as a man can ask for,
a place to start.

Conference at Chaffey's Locks

(sunfish that will not come to my hand
an oriole in a silver birch
stars flying past me in the dark)

I speak and you speak
and I try to discover
a country to inhabit
in your words or my own.

(an inverted white boat
lying by the water
and reflected below

boat and image
floating image and boat)

The price of silence
is always silence.

I will buy gifts
to take home to my children.

Flying

Maggie is seven now
and nearly eight,
is wide-blue-eyed, noisy,
difficult, tactless,
incapable of lying
(even to save a life, I think)
in most things
all too much
like her Praise-God-Barebones father.

She now and then
pulls petals from a daisy
and says "He loves me, loves me not,"
although I'm not sure
she cares much yet.

And this evening once again
she looks up from reading
flaps her arms
and says "Did I fly a little?"

I explain for the hundredth time
the task's impossible,
that no-one can ever do it.

She says she knows
and tries again and says
"I can land better. Maybe
I can't learn how to fly,
but I can learn to land."

I doubt that too,
but looking at her,
her wild hair and bright eyes,

I smile and say yes.

Reading

In the still light
of our morning house
Kate sits beside me
as we read a book.

The pictures are familiar
and at the far end
of memory, I see them
and me at six or seven
in the small house
on a Toronto street
where the child mysteries lived
that I lived with,
and the child fears
born of darkness
and not yet being
accustomed to living.

I was afraid of my father,
a man perhaps gentler
than I can be.
My children cringe at my rages.

And soon enough
I will embarrass them
with my foolish jokes
old puns, clown dances.
They will soon grow up
and find me childish.

Even now when I walk
in Maggie's school
I am a child in the maze
of starting to be,
where the boys
flaunted their hard-ons
and I lost a tooth
playing floor hockey.

I recognize myself
by that hole in my mouth.

Maybe as we get older
the brain gets more and more
full of the past
until there's no room
for things to happen
and nothing does.

If so, the best wisdom
is forgetfulness, the saint
an amnesiac.

I will cultivate
my absent-mindedness
but can I ever forget
why I have a missing tooth
and not know
where I lived?

That we are and are not
is an old truth,
and the sun tomorrow
may move from west to east,
but I wouldn't bet on it.

If we run out of new books to read
I can always write one.

Cartoons

The children sit, awkward, graceful
in their bodies, curled
in an old chair or on the rug,
their eyes not seeing me watching.

Their hair hangs in morning tangles,
clothes mismatched, rumpled with sleep
as they stare into the flat world
to watch the endless chases,
the dynamite, blows, falls, floods
that do not stop the automaton predators.
The cartoon god's grace
protects the audacious bird or mouse.

The fox, wolf, dog
overleap and fall, shattering,
always lose, collapse, break,
put themselves back together,
too stupid to know they'll never win,
having this much of perfection.

Outside the window
sun grins on the ice.

CND Festival of Life

Bethnal Green, Easter 1970

A crowd is moving
toward the park
and men and women
touched by hope or curiosity
are walking over the grass.

The spontaneous music
will begin at 4.30.

My daughter Kate who loves
all jewelry lays claim
to a disarmer's emblem pin
found in the mud.

A sudden rush
of angry boys
thrusts past. We reach
for the children.

There is electric music
in the air as we walk
under the trees and past
a game of volleyball.

We eat lemon ices
and end the day
in momentary sunlight
among the boys and girls
and Sunday families rowing
on a crowded pond.

I steer the boat
carefully among them
as we all move
over the shallow water.

The ducks swim past
and fly away, return
all around us. The day
grows dark. I turn our boat
to the shore of Bethnal Green.

Apparitions: for George and Lenna

Between your house and the lake
the sour red cherries
hang like blood
among the dark green leaves.

A spirit in your house
breathes, walks, closes doors.
And Lenna told how her sister
was bitten by a voodoo snake.

(Grass moving. The men saw the grass move.

The voodoo doctor's woman
had sympathy, said Oh, Oh,
the child, she is too young,
and took the snake on herself.

Child crying, Oh the snake,
the snake, get it off me.
The snake was invisible
but blood came from its bites.)

The puppies under the porch howl.
The children catch a white one
and bring it out. All the children
have lovely eyes.

(While our backs were turned,
the cherry trees walked to the lake
and drowned their blood-red fruit.)

This House

In the back shed, the guinea pig
squeaks demanding food.
The cage is nearly filled
with its brown droppings.

In the bathroom, the floor oozes
a dark and nasty liquid; most
of the chairs in the house
are broken, unfit to sit on.

The hungry dog drools as we eat.
The back porch is rotting
and falling apart, the garden
is nothing but dying weeds.

Hallowe'en pumpkins leer,
and on the wall, dozens
of mounted butterfly wings
define the shape of the air.

Maggie's shoes smell
of horses, and when Kate
sets her pen on paper,
a monster begins to grow.

The porch is full of leaves.
All of the taps are dripping.
Whoever you are that knocks,
come in, come in.

The Barn

It's always part of the background,
the worn walls of a strange green.
It sits there at the edge of the yard,
six inches onto the neighbour's land,
the board and batten walls making it seem
higher, thinner. I see it each day
from the kitchen window. If I walk up
the street toward the house,
it's there behind the lilacs.
On winter mornings when I come
around the back to get the car,
it's there across the yard, rising
out of the snow drifts.
                            Inside,
darkness, a confusion of old furniture,
papers, tools, boxes of screws and bolts
left by the previous owner,
the mud nests of wasps, old toys,
suitcases of worn-out clothes.
                            In summer
the children hide away upstairs,
dress in those clothes, and sometimes say
the words they don't dare say outdoors.

I've often made plans for the future,
to do something with the place,
to make it lighter, cleaner,
throw out the last of the clutter, make
a pleasant retreat across the yard
where I could work or in the warm weather
someone could live.

                    But this morning,
seeing it there in the snow, green,
high and still, peaked, faded, it was
too much too beautiful.
                    I sat still
in the car seat and looked at the old place
and didn't plan any changes at all.

Day, Night

In the wild sunflowers
yellow becomes a dimension,
a way of seeing, a yellow
beyond yellow, at the top
of a spindly stem.

At night sometimes I find
women so lovely so young
it hurts to see them.

The sunflower calyx repeats
itself in yellow and brown
to make a clustered seedbed.
The thirteen petals are pointed
like the disc of the sun.

In their eyes at night
I see fear, joy and the longing
to be held, to be hurt.

At night I fall in love
with everyone, love becomes
a dimension, a way of seeing.

Peter's Farm

The wasps hum as they rise and fall,
move in and out in the sunlight
that pours over the old barn,
the wasps rising, falling, like
the figures of an antique dream
or dancers of an ancient dance,

so simple in their insect glory
in the September sunlight. I watch
as they fly in and out and fall
to the ground (and only hours later
wonder why they fall, if already
their dazed hard pattern has closed).

As we talk, I lie on my back
in the green grass and look
into the air. I see a hawk
moving slowly, so slowly, like
a slow finger writing on the sky
in an old lost language.

The cattle too seem like the figures
of a painting, a relief, the daughters
of the September sun that stalls
and broods over the fields heavy
with flowers; wasps, hawk, cattle
dreaming themselves through the halls of sleep.

Our voices as we sit, my friend and I,
and talk about what must be talked about,
cannot attain the calm, the simpleness
of wasp or hawk or cattle, and the earth
is pestered from the fulness of its dream
by the voice of our desires, our remorse.

Poem for the Lintel of Wuthering Heights

Who loves must let his lover set
his house on fire yet make it stand,
must feel his heart within and yet
must see it burning in his hand.

Men say the windows of the soul
are only mirrors giving back
a love that cannot make us whole;
we never find the thing we lack.

And time and love are still at war.
Silence still falls on man and wife.
What will you find beyond this door?
A house of death. A house of life.

Light does all the trick
of making beauty. Here the light
lies on the surface
of the river, on the movement
of the surface of the water
as light creates the surface
and the river slides past.

(A woman said "He's getting old,
and he isn't very brave.")

From over the river I can hear
voices of children, almost
hear them, almost imagine
that they are part of the wind
but hear them, not see them,
see nothing but the trees.

(For a second the landscape
staggers like a wounded man
under the weight of memory.
Holds very still, rights itself.
Trees again endure the air.

A woman said to me "He's getting old,
and he isn't very brave.")

Now all the words we said
are gone into the air,
are said, are gone.
They are on the far side
of everything. The words
we speak are going
as we say them.

Where are they, these children
whose voices I can hear?

I look into the empty woods,
see nothing, hear them, still.
The voices. The voices.

The Children

We made them in the night,
unknowing, riding into time,
our minds on love or pleasure
or the darkness of the dark.

They were always unintended,
like beauty or like joy,
yet now they are my life
and time and place of being.

They are riding into time
on the dangerous ships of love.
They are riding into time,
into dark, into themselves.

We made them in the night,
and at the end we leave them,
leave them riding into time
in the darkness of the dark.

Now in late afternoon
the October leaves
are no longer colours
but only light.

As they go
toward the end
of their time
they become
transparent.

Tasting the gently
bitter taste
of afternoons
that go on
like this
and on like
this,

I would be light,
silence, not
to be, only
to be transparent,
a moving absence

a silence
at the heart
of silence.

Old Man, Young Lady

I'd seen him hitchhiking here before
in his long coat, with his sack.
I offered him a box of cookies,
he took them, held them with the wrist
of his paralyzed hand as his fingers
shoved them one by one
through his heavy beard.

He told me he'd been travelling
for 36 years.
Worked at farming until he lost
the use of his hand,
now travelled summer and winter.

Said he'd slept out the night before
and might again tonight. He had
an extra coat he used to cover his feet.

I dropped him off where we turned
and he made a joke, said he'd take
one of my girls along with him.
We drove into the October afternoon
and came to the farm.

> Lady in the blue photograph,
> living at the edge of blue
> in the blue tree, in the sky,
> lady, living in the moment
> of the camera or running into the air,
> the blue air, into the water,
> lady living in a book with blue pages
> and pale blue letters, I can see
> only the shadow of blue, your eyes
> that are moving somewhere
> at the edge of my darkness.

Kate and I stood in the yard
and watched the horses move
through the cold and falling dark.
The world expanded like a breathing lung.
Black fingers of trees reached up
against the last light. The breath
of the horses was steam in the air.

I wondered where the old man
was meeting this darkness,
whether the lights of passing cars
suddenly caught him
at the side of the highway,
caught him and passed him.
I wondered if he would wake alone
in a place of frosted grass.

> Lady turning at the edge of grey,
> speaking at the edge of shadow, lady
> appearing between the frames
> of movies, between the lines
> of poems, lady of words, lady
> of silence, I can only hear
> the colour of your shadow
> between your words.

Coming back it was night
and we followed the road
returning in a maze of trucks
and moving cars and lights
that wove the darkness into journeys.

The lovely trees and hills had gone
under the surface of the mind.
The car destroyed the miles of distance.

And at the end the children
sang out with joy
to see the glittering lights
of the city.

A Moving Window

The light of the November afternoon
slanting across the fields
catching weed, weedflower, branch, twig,
is a kind of blossoming.

The woods beside the road
are woven into a tapestry
by the falling light. The moon
waits, white and patient, for the night.

Empire of day, empire of night,
sun, moon, a momentary beauty;
I am riding toward a house
that no longer seems my own.

Now and always there are limits drawn
around my loving. The November flowering
is the limit of this day's beauty.
At its end come only possibilities.

Drunken Poem

Afternoon is invading my eyes.
Between here and the barn
the fallen leaves lie untouched.
I never rake the lawn, I never
clean the car. The children
squabble all round me
as the day darkens and beer
darkens my brain and the thought
of you and a thousand confusions
darken my heart, and I find
a photograph on the table
of a newborn child. My child, I think,
my Kate who now stands near me,
grown, difficult, beloved, and I find
the threat of tears invading my eyes.

Oh sentimental absurd man, who
can you think you are, writing
this something, nothing, drunken words
that solve nothing and say
nothing, only that I know
nothing and that the earth
is the body of a god and you
and I are the body of a god.

The children laugh. I remember
the night that Kate was born.

All afternoon I have said to myself
that love is too simple, is only
an easy death. I think of the men
and women who are puzzled at me
and what they have heard me say.

I am the eyes of god, I am
the tongue of god and so are you
and you and you, even dying,
even hating the world to death.

Rhetoric, beer rhetoric, I have nothing
to claim but a willingness to lose.

I wear a child's Indian headdress.
I write with a ball-point pen.
My brain is addled by beer,
by the coming of dark, by the love
of death, by you, by all the times
that I didn't know what I was doing.

The trees are black against the blue air
as the paper boy does his rounds
and the day becomes gone. Time,
death, loving; we can only live
by being in love with loss, with disaster.

There is no conclusion to this poem. Ever.

Three Haiku

Your hair is an old
darkness and sometimes we both
are lost inside it.

Your wrists and ankles
are thin as bird bones; they make
all thoughts return small.

Skin is where you touch
the wind, water and all things
that are your lovers.

The Silver Bird

The bird has no desire
to fly, only the silver
wings that lift it
to a place of light.

The bird is a destiny
of silver, feathered
with light and flying
on no wind in no air
upward, upward
until the earth is far
and curved and the whole
round earth bends
into the shining eyes
and the brain
holds the silver world
like a secret.

The bird has no desire
only the silver wings
and a destiny of light.

Snow, this snow
the flakes repeated
in the darkening blue
afternoon. The seeing
is calmly, blessedly
perfect. Words are not
enough for this,
the words are not blue
enough nor quiet enough.

Below me, the dark
figures move, silent,
moving past the tall
poplars that reach
upward to where I am.

Say I could hold
in my hand the silence,
the blue, this moment,
say I could hold out
to you only this,
not the words, but
only the desire
for the words, this
snow, the afternoon.

Here in my hand
not the words, only
this. This. This.

The figures at the bottom
of the hill, blue and green
and red in the white field
of snow, are my children.

They don't look real
far down there in the white
reach of the snow. Are small
as the images of memory,

as if I were watching
myself in the white fields
of the past, the world
all far away and small.

> (What is present is
> the present and what
> I remember, the jewel
> against your skin,
> a dress, the moment
> tied in a knot
> of flesh and bones
> is now a memory,
> a possible fact.)

The image of my child self
turns to inquire. The small
boy asks from too far away.
I cannot answer him.

I sent him back. Look down
through the thousand flakes
of snow that fall and fall
from the thick grey sky.

From the bottom of the hill,
pulling their toboggan,
the small figures, blue, green,
red, climb up toward me.

Lessons

1

This was the history
of the time, the first
settlements, precarious,
tentative, hanging
on the edge of dark,

then ships (like words
like tongues of light)
appeared on the water;

we settled a few
miles of lost country,
set the touch of hands
against the forest;

now we are here, but don't
know quite where we are.

2

The children stand
at the windows
tracing maps,
the coloured shapes
of the far countries.

The books tell them
of size, rainfall,
products, local customs,

but do not say
"If you come here
you will find
only what you make.
You will travel
only as far
as you dare to imagine."

3

I could draw a map
of your body, write
a history of your acts,

chart the scar
at the end of your nose,

record the movement
of your breath in my mouth,

but all this would be
a little beside the point

now that we've moved on
to learning languages.

The evergreen trees
are dressed in their ghosts,
each holds a white echo
of its shape.

A white figure
whirls and explodes
in the air,
here, gone, darkness.

In the morning, drifts
are the shape of wind,
a ghost of the night.

We are all dressed
in ghosts, you and I
and all lovers, wearing
the shapes of other
bodies on our own.

Sometimes we turn and see
an unknown look on a face
we thought we knew
and recognize the presence
of a lover's ghost
until it vanishes
and the face
is only the face
we thought we knew.

Sometimes at night
I am dressed in the ghost
of you as if in snow,
and at the moment
when the ghost leaves,
peels itself from my skin,
I know, almost know,
feel that somewhere
in the windsweep white
snow world lying
under the dark wind,
my snow ghost is dancing
hand in pale hand
with yours.

Seeing

Late in the January afternoon
I sat alone at the kitchen table,
finished a glass of beer and turned
the bottom of the glass to the sun.

And made the circles of glass burn
in rings, concentric bright blinding
rings of light.
                      And stared
into the glass where the sun
broke apart, as if I could find
in that wreckage of light an image
that would tell me everything.

(When I told you this, you remembered
rings of air you sometimes see, looking
up from a book and toward a window, seeing
moving rings of air.)
                             Rings of light,
rings of air; and on the wall
beside my shadow now, the light moves
in ripples, and on the near corner
of the paper where I write this, a pattern
of streaks and clouds.
                          The almost invisible
shapes of transparency shadow the room.

At times like this, the beloved world
is shaken in flashes of light, patterns,
ripples, illusions built in the air
by the need to see.
                      I hold my glass
to the light, and the round bubbles
in the beer float upward, shining.

Light is a fire
at the edge of the invisible,
an illusion built in the eye
by the need to see.
                      (Oh woman,
illusion of my blinded eyes, see
the man you built of rings of air,
the man you built to fill the space
between your eyes and the light,
see how he turns a glass to the sun,
to make again the flashing rings,
the painful rings of light.)

You tell me, tell me
lost and hidden words
for I am the secret
childhood;
   you tell
me, denying, denying;
you shine like
polished bone, your eyes
meet me, I look back,
wanting to drive them
inward to fall
like trash in your brain
where the skull flashes
electric sparks, short
circuits across the grey
clouds of denial.
    I would
dress you in your secret
body, do damage,
oh child-heart, to the trash
and cinders in your head.

Teacher-child, the tools
of my crime are fire
and a knife of light.

My fingers are on
the balls of your eyes,
pressing them in away
from seeing,
    the babble
of your wet mouth
falls into dream;

the knives of my body
edged with fire
are quick to cut
into your secret flesh
for I am only
gentle in words, am
the devil surgeon
cutting you in pieces;
I am the secret secret
that the nerved
steel soft fire
of your womb
caressed.
        I am
the assassin
of all your disguises.

Report from the City of Dreams

Where I've never been, Vancouver
where I was going to go
to see the mountains and the ocean

A woman has come back
to tell me about the lonely people
asking for things
              how it is greyer
and sadder than England
                  that a friend
who lives there now spends all his time
watching TV
            that the streets are full
of lonely people
            Oh she hated the place
and one of the poems of her life
fell into nothing there

Where I've never been
              where sea
and mountains and the poets have made
a city of dreams
            the end of the road west
edge of the sea

            A city full of poets
a dozen gangs who walk the streets
calling out insults
        "Hey you
fat motherfucker bad poet, come out
and fight"
        And sometimes at night
meet in the centre of the city's
imagination and fight it out
and in the morning piles of dead poems
lie like dog shit in the streets

I've decided not to go there
to travel east, not west, to go down
to the seacoast where nothing is ever
expected, where the cities are built
of bitter memories, where the future
is something not to think about
where the seaports look back to Europe
without hope or regret
      I'll go in summer
when the good weather comes, and the kids
take to the highway, a generation of poets
chasing metaphors, up to TO, out to Van
down to California, finding at the end
of the trip that the man on their back
came along for the ride, that he's a poet too
and can never get his fill of their metaphors
eats them by bushels and asks for more

    Night cities
    cities of bone
architectures of stone and longing
    cities of windows
  of empty streetcars
    lunar cities
    under the sea
and on the mountaintops
    buried cities
  where kings ate death
    cities of gardens
  haunted by madmen
architectures of stone and regret
    cities
    dream cities

We travel to see them or hear from friends
travelling alone or together the long roads
of the country
    I hardly care now
    if I ever see Vancouver

Parmenides Among the Lost

                Turning I saw
a figure standing in the doorway
in the dark. Turning I see
time turn again.
                  The Bobbsey twins
are always twelve, my daughter says.
All their adventures happen in one
eternal year where time is stayed
as still as the broken china swan
I remade in my hand, the grip
of my fingers awkward on the thin
small fragments that I set together,
holding the curving neck in place
with a steel pin, glueing the pieces
of white china into the regained shape
of a tiny swan, so small, so brittle
that I could crush it into bits.

So call this now the eternal year
of the china swan, the year
of figures at the door of darkness,
of the little boat of Tu Fu that moved
through his poems on a flood of memories
as the poet grew old
                  & at last died
on his boat
          & perhaps it floated
away, free of the poet's hand, rocking
& tossing like the shadow of a dying
waterfowl on the flooded Yangtse,
a withered body on deck.

Turning

I saw a figure by the door
in a blue nightgown in the cold,
watching me as I waited in the snow
for a cab to come
                    & that figure
like every figure we turn and see
behind us, stood at the door
of an eternal year where the Bobbsey twins
solve every mystery except the puzzle
of why they never grow up
                    & the boat
of Tu Fu that was lost in the flood
1200 years ago is afloat
in the winter sky among the constellations

& everything is true.

Cold Saturday

1

I stood at the counter
of the children's library
while a young girl
prepared the books.

On the counter was taped a card
with the message "WATCH
FOR ANGELICO LOPEZ, QUEEN STREET,"
and the instruction to check
carefully all his books
for torn-out pages.

Down in the streets
below the window
the cars moved slowly
through the snow. The air
was all snow moving, drifting,
filling the city streets.

The message wrote itself
on the wind and called out
to the whole city
WATCH FOR ANGELICO LOPEZ
QUEEN STREET.
               Men and women
standing in the post-office lobby
for warmth couldn't quite hear it.

2

Maggie and I saw the gull
in a crevice between the rocks,
its wing held awkwardly
behind it and frozen

into the ice at the edge
of the cold green lake.

We looked down
at a glittering bright eye
that looked back.

We had only one pair
of gloves between us.
I took them and bent
to the frightened bird
and pulled its wing
from the grip of ice.

The gull turned its beak
to me and opened it
in a futile threat,
then flopped forward
onto the ice.

Lay there helpless,
and I hadn't the faith
or strength or skill
to save it and asked
my young child
if I should kill it.

Yes, she said, but she
didn't want to watch.

I went down the shore
to find a lethal rock
or stick but found none,
and when I came back
the bird had made its way
to the water and dropped
into the cold green lake
among the chunks of ice.

We turned away
and as we walked along
I looked at the lake
and saw the gull
swimming out into the cold
dragging one wing.

3

The room, the window, the boy,
outside, the blowing snow,
the boy sitting by the window
of the room with a book.

Outside the traffic moves
one way on a one-way street
but quiet today, the snow
stopping the noise, the boy

sits quietly looking through
the pages of the book,
searching, perhaps not yet
sure what it is he wants.

Behind him the Saturday noises,
brothers, sisters, games
and arguments, and the boy
finds the page he wants,

the right page somehow, no-one
else will ever know why,
but the right page, and he tears
it roughly out of the book.

4

WATCH FOR ANGELICO LOPEZ
THE UNOFFICIAL EDITOR
IS LOOSE IN THE BOOK OF LIFE

WATCH FOR ANGELICO LOPEZ
PAGE AFTER PAGE IS VANISHING
THE BOOK OF LIFE IS GOING

WATCH FOR HIM BEWARE BEWARE
WATCH FOR ANGELICO LOPEZ

5

Boy stands frozen in the eye
of Librarian. Looks through him.
Looks through the book. The page
is gone. Torn out. Anger
rises over him like a weapon.

His eye bright, defiant. He watches
unmoved as she takes the card
that allows him books. Tears it.
He moves away. Leaves her crippled.

6

The notebook
where I write this
has poems from Spain
(red, orange)
poems from England
(grey, grey)
and some more recent
(silver, blue).

I can look
at the pages and see
my words grow
into poems,
the sight
of what I saw
the sound
of what I felt
recorded here.
But the times
I wrote about
are gone.

All the living die,
everything vanishes
but words, all
but the poems.
          Only
the pages of books
endure.

This poem is only for now,
a moment, like a cigarette
or a glass of beer or a room
you're glad to be in.

This poem is only some words
to say for now, like this,
like a face seen from a bus
or in a restaurant, or even

a thought that you didn't know
was in your mind until
you thought it, and it was.
This poem is not for a lifetime,

for books, for talking about,
but only for now, like a foolish
gift that solves nothing and leaves
the vacuum of solitude untouched.

This poem is useless as the touch
of my hand, a gesture out of the need
to make a gesture, like the words
of saying this poem is only for now.

Found Poems

1

The stains on this garment
have not been overlooked.
We feel to process further
might result in injury
to the colour and fabric.

2

Hot Pants

1/3 Off

Stopping on Ice

        Suddenly
                he was down—
his eyes strange, someone said,
mouth open—
            42 years old
coming back once a year
to the boys' game
                for charity,
a red-faced man with children
and a job and a mortgage.

                In 1949
he spent a playoff in the NHL
and that was as far as he got
in hockey
        but he died on the ice, seen
by 2000 people
             each one
catching a different angle
                      a different moment,
their eyes drawn away from the puck
converging like rays of light
on the broken moment
                  of his falling
2000 images
          laid
one on top of the other so that
I see him falling
              over and over
going down in slow
                motion

            his face
                  like the boy's face
            in tomorrow's newspaper, an Old Timer
            playing for charity
                              passing the goal
            reaching for the post
                              missing
                                          coasting
            on out near the blue line
                                    sinking
            to his knees
                        and reaching out
            and falling—
                        4000 eyes
            seeing a boy who had his kidney
            pierced by a skate at sixteen—
                                          the red face
            of the man darkening, sinking, gone now
            as he fell to the silver ice
                                    slowly
            2000 times
                        like a boy
            falling
                  and dying.

Audubon

1

The night that he was born
the midwife cried out
"Look, look, his little thing,
how it is like a bird,
beaked and bare,
huddled down in its nest
and look, already
how it tries to fly."

2

He walked and paddled
through a thousand miles
of bush, a tapestry
of earth, leaves, sky, leaves, earth,
where he saw birds
that no-one else could see.

Later, in a studio
full of dead birds,
skins and feathers,
stuffed birds with glass eyes,
assistants would draw in
the branches or flowers,
the misty landscapes,
but always at the centre
his own work
in pairs, male and female,
lark or dove or hawk or thrush.

3

When they came
to close the coffin
they saw the feathers
as they began to sprout
at the shoulders.
They stood back watching
as the pinions grew
lifting the body
from the wooden box.
They watched, astonished,
as he rose and spread his wings,
flew out the door
and past the trees,
soaring and falling,
crying out in the languages
of his birds, flew onward
and would not ascend to heaven.

The Song of the Dream Fish

I am unknown, unless
you look down in a sleeping
moment into tenebrous
pools where all falling

stops and deepens. Look
twice and you lose me.
I am momentary, shining,
slippery as love,

I glow down at the back
of your brain too. I swim
the canals of the spine
and through the molecules

of your soft flesh.
I move slow in the still
water of your cells,
pulsing like the sun.

In all the fluids
of your changing,
this my luminous body
returns like sleep.

Heathcliff as a Spaceman

The blessed ones always moving
    & falling outward
left their presence in the streets
    of Liverpool
in the flesh of this gypsy brat
    spawn of dark
sailor and Liverpool Welsh Druid
    whore
        & falling
inside the story of that dark
    sailor, they made
a man come into the shape of action
    the ship moving
always outward toward some final disaster
    a terminus
of the world.   The blessed ones
come thus through space in the invisible
    wingless cars of light
& set down stories we must learn
    to be
        & falling
into our lives, day by day, strangers,
    ambassadors, speak.

    The boy forgot
the star voyage, the scope of space
    & falling through
the Liverpool alleys, thought his rage
    was against hunger
& cold: memory blind as walls.

    But the girl too
had been left, child in the hills,
    at a sudden encounter
of the visible and invisible along
    a crack in time
where the fit of past to future was rough
    & the impossible
coming occurred.
               & he wondered only once
    in the moment of dying
if all time was always shattered
    & if the chariots
of the blessed ones were forever arriving
    in the open years
& falling into what we are.

    Until then he saw
only the sister-child-stranger's
    almost transparency
& thought that if he could beat through
    the wall of flesh,
world would drop into the eventual
    endless falling,
a wingless dumb flight upward
    across the distanceless
lost ranges of space
               & into the hands,
    the solitary light
hands of the blessed ones
               & at that
    moment of falling
the dark sailor who had been made
    to be his father
would sail off the edge of the world
    into the multiple
unreal returnings of infinite lost stories.

         white sails in mist)

(and sunlight
silver on water
              white
sails
     moving
in the echo of white
on white

         (the boats
         sail on
         in the summer
         of my eyes)

and you)

         (pale luminous
         moving away)

the island almost
invisible

         the boats
are gone

         (the sky

Notes for a Wedding Song

1

listen again, listen
to the speech of water
of trees

at the edge
where the city reaches
its end at water

behind me
          and away
the city is small
under a painted sky

the water speaks, trees
speak, wind gives
its motion, words

watching the painted city, say
no city is ever real

2

in a room

        the placing of chairs
        an expectation

a choice of windows

outside there is only
and always

        weather and events
        news of other countries

Passing the Cathedral

She has one man on each side,
a pair of temporary wings;
she is brought down the steps
and moved to a waiting car.

October rains on her widowhood.

The huge sensual gift
has abandoned a man
who walked beside her
on one side only.

Now she is symmetrical,
one man on each side.
Now she is alone.

Hallowe'en Sunday

A river is the music
of water
        and in it shining
falls to music and dead leaves
are as bright in water as in air.

Today again the return of all this
repetitive yearly adventure
so stirs the heart that I can see
all the shining of the world
in the single flash of a moment's
light on the moving of the water.

And my hand against your hand,
the surface of my world touching
the surface of yours makes
all rivers, the falling into all rivers
even what is lost in the depth
of the music of river and light, enough.

And we throw our hats into the water.

Photograph of a Room

It's all a matter of sunlight
of your sweater
     an odd
green colour
     your back toward me
& the winter sun coming at an angle
into the warm room.

A pan sits on the stove
& just over the edge of the counter
a piece of silver foil
half crumpled.
     It's all a matter
of your hair, unbrushed, still damp
from the shower.
     (Voices
& music come from below
where a country-and-western singer
retired at 22, lives with her man
& another man's child.)
     Outside
where stone and snow shape light
a church bell rings.
     It's all a matter
of being able to say
that the sunlight on your shoulder
was bright
    & the sound of your pen
defined the shape of my hearing.

Disappearances

Seeing you, a distance
beyond touching, hearing
your voice in the dark,
seeing you across the space
of a room talking to strangers,
I disappear into knowing
that you are far off
and all new.

Seeing you, a distance
beyond touching,
my hesitant unknowing eyes
watch your soft familiar mouth
moving in prayer.

And I look away.

Here in the warm yellow
light of a room
if I turn my head
just to the left
there is a blue window.

Outside is everything
that is not inside
i.e., snow, buildings,
streets, cars, a lake,
someone with your name.

Looking out the window
into the blue world
I can see the black
windows of an empty building.
The windows are opaque
but somewhere behind
may be a man, looking
from inside at everything
that is not inside.

(A camera is a conquering window
that turns time into space,
light into shape;
the windows of the head
are victims of time and light.)

Inside a warm room, I see
the snow blowing, the night
darkening the window's blue
depth until it is only
blackness reflecting
the light of the room.

Outside in the dark
is everything
that is not inside
i.e., snow, buildings,
streets, cars, a lake,
someone with your face.

The snow is never pure for long;
within moments of its falling
a man will walk out
from a doorway somewhere
and his footsteps will break the level
white curves of the surface.
                                      Or a dog
or cat will move, relieve itself, move on
and gradually, step after step,
the simple whiteness vanishes into a complex
record of what has passed.

                                    Nothing is pure
for longer. There is that imaginary
second when anything is perfect
but of course that has never happened.
The footsteps are always beginning somewhere.

And love is not a presence but a history.

Heraldry

The map is coloured with names
as magical as schoolbooks,
Chartres, Valois, Aquitaine, Anjou,
and the colours unroll a tapestry,
the Black Prince at his battlefield,
Harold at Hastings with the arrow
splitting his eye,
         Jehanne, la bonne Lorraine,
or maistre François himself
                    in winter
in a landscape of kings and horses,
Poitiers (the horses rear), Orléans,
the crossbows set free their arrows
that scatter like shafts of light.

                    Morning
today was the landscape of a house
in ruins, dirty socks, coffee cups, glasses,
remnants of our loving drunken night,
disorderly, dim.

              The Black Prince
enters the fields of Aquitaine, his horse
black, his eyes black.
                 A peasant girl
sits in a field of flowers, rocking stupidly
and singing in a monotone.

                    Outside
the morning was almost warm, the snow melting,
air smelling of the streets and earth.
After the hot darkness of night and loving
it was hard to keep my feet on the ground
in so much light.

                    Maistre François
clerk, student, thief, rises from bed
shivering, and the tapestry grins mouths
of wolves. Wolves in the streets
of Paris.
            (Valois, Beauvais, Poitiers,
cities that speak in flags
and men at arms.)
                        The figures move on
in the flat world of their weaving,
the coloured threads loomed or stitched
into a map of time; here is yellow, here
red and here green, but in the next
century, the colours shift,
the dukes exchange their castles.

All our music is heard at a distance
the horses seen far off
at twilight in snow, seen in passing
and lost.
            Darkness heats
in our bodies like food; we eat
and drink and love as carelessly
as dogs.

(The mutinous soldiers move
through the fields in sullen groups.
They seize the peasant girl and tear
her flesh in pieces.)

Harriet Shelley at the Serpentine

There is a smell of morning here. The grass
of the park is watching me. Nothing moves.
When I look up at the clouds
I do not believe in the sky. Beyond them
only more clouds. If the sun
shone on me now, I would disappear,
perhaps melt.
                 Somewhere, if I wait,
something will move, and it will come
toward me.
             All my life, waiting—
I thought he brought it then,
but he only gave me this—morning
by the Serpentine, the grass damp
and the grey clouds seen in the grey water
leaving no space between sky and earth.

Is this poetry, this confusion?
Perhaps this has a meaning. After it all
this is what I waited for.
                     No wonder
my sister wished me to buy clothes,
silver, a carriage.
              If this is poetry,
if this is the end of what he had to say—
his soft eyes, they cried out how unfair
my father was to me. Cried out
and his eyes were like a fire,
                     and I thought
How have I deserved this? Harriet,
simple pretty Harriet?
                Clever, he said,
but I knew I wasn't. He loved me
and wanted me to be clever for him
to love. I could see this, simple
as I am.

       Saw too much. Now stand
at the Serpentine shivering on this December
morning. Alone. I knew, but would not
believe it. That I would be left alone.
I could see in his soft eyes that he
would tire of thinking me clever.
                            Blamed
my sister, poor man, could not think
that I was only poor simple Harriet,
his pretty harmless girl.
                   As I look
down into the water, I feel its depth
I will sink down.

                He said as he lay
in me that I was a little boat,
and he set sail in this
across the oceans of light. His words
were lovely when he told me this,
but when he said "Here. Here is a poem"
my poor mind broke apart into fear
and useless memories.
                    In Italy
I think it is warm now. He told me this.
She holds him. She thinks how sad
and wonderful and gay and kind
he is. She thinks my thoughts now.
I am no longer on the earth. England
is the empty shell he left behind.
I am his ghost.

             Still nothing moves
except the child in my belly.
How happy he was that night, coming
to say goodbye, to say
he would always be my friend.
He touched my face, and I was glad
that he was with me and pleased
to comfort me.

                And I was glad
that last time in my life
I made him happy.
                    Our lips
needed only to touch, and nothing
would ever happen again. His touch
ran over my skin like light across water.
He loved me and wept.
                      I chose
to believe him for that was what I meant
by love.
          I have no thoughts.
I am his ghost. My name
is Smith. I am anonymous.
My children are memories of him.
The one that grows in me moves
quietly in the anonymous womb
of Mrs. Smith. Who stands here at the edge
of the grey water.
                I am his ghost,
and this my act is another of his poems.

The Best Name of Silence

1

BLUEBEARD: I have never been anything
at all. My name
is your name, and you
are what I will be
if I must be.
My voice
is your secret voice.

I am the mask you wear
but cannot see.

I am pain.

2

VOICES: Nothing will grow in his earth.

He sleeps on sheets made of human skin.

His body is a mistake.

He has the breasts of a woman.

Animals run from him. Birds fly from him.

He has tasted forbidden knowledge.

He has eaten the flesh of children.

His gaze can drive men mad.

These things have not been seen.
These things are true
because we have all said them.

3

BLUEBEARD: The caves of earth:
light of the phosphorescent
plants, the smell
of pale mushrooms,
vegetable decay.

Flies dance and fall
to the wet floor where
iridescent green and blue
and gold-black beetles attend.

Deeper, further on,
the ferns. No colour.
Somewhere ahead, she moves.
I can hear the sound.

4

GIRL: One childhood morning when I woke
my dreams held me, and I
was awake yet not awake.
I moved slowly as if my legs
were moving in water. The light
was strangely green, and I thought
that I was at the bottom
of the ocean; the birds
moved slowly through the air
like bright fishes.

I walked through trees
that seemed to wave in air
like weeds under the sea.

When I returned to the house
I stood in green sunlight
in the yard and stared
at the doorway. I knew
there was a place
I must go to, but was a child
and could not go there.

The geese in the yard
were still and white.
Their long necks reached
and bent toward me.
I was at the centre and afraid.

5

VOICES: This face is a trap.

>   The eyes do not blink.
>   The beard is blue.
>
>   The face is dark suffused
>   red, almost purple;
>   there is something of stale
>   blood broods in the colour.
>
>   The head is bare, bald,
>   shining like water.
>
>   The eyes are lost
>   in the bone caves
>   and the lapped layers
>   of skin, the seamed
>   and wrinkled bags of eyelids.
>
>   The face is sealed.
>   It is a trap.

The teeth are dark
and sharp.

The eyes do not blink
Stale blood sags
in the skin.

6

GIRL: His mouth is saying
his treasures, gold, silver
ruby, lace, ivory.

Yet there is a smell
of earth in his words.

BLUEBEARD: She listens only
to my words, she
does not hear
the voice of my need.

GIRL: He tries to hide
his face from me,
sits awkwardly
half sideways,
but I can look at him
easily. I have never
been frightened
of toads or beetles.

BLUEBEARD: I speak of her beauty
but that is not
what I mean to say.
There is more to beauty
than beauty. My voice
screams in my head.

GIRL: Something is happening
to the air. I seem
to taste the light.
On the wall two flies
are locked together.
Something is happening.

BLUEBEARD: I must not turn
and let her see
my eyes. I don't know
what they would show
but she must not see it.

GIRL: I have never dared
to ask questions. I wish
for this to end.

    I wonder what marriage
will be like.

7

VOICES: We are the voice
of the commonwealth.
Our bodies bend
at the joints.

    We will allow
what is allowable.

We are the voice
of the past.
Our eyes look
both ways.

    We are the witnesses
of the ceremony.

We are the voice
of the future.
Our actions
only happen.

    When this is over
    we will say it is done.

8

BLUEBEARD: Aaah ... aaah ....

    Pale dawn light touches her.
    I cannot keep it off, the lecherous
    light strokes her skin.

    Her fine pale skin
    that holds in the red
    blood, guts, spleen,
    liver, womb, the little
    rhythmic heart; pulse, pulse.
    There at the neck
    an artery, pulse, pulse.

    The lecherous light covers
    her and makes her shine.

    Aaah ... aaah ....

    There and there and there too.

    One, two, three, four, five ... and
      another ....

    Seven.

    Aaah ... aaah ....

Seven hairs from my beard,
seven blue hairs lie curled
On her skin, shine
on the pallid and shimmering
whiteness. Her. Seven, seven
blue hairs shining in the dawn,
one by the pale nipple
of her left breast, one
clinging somehow at the side
of her thin throat, another
just here by her navel, one
below that in the pale
brown curls. Here and here
on the round fleshed thighs
and on her face by lips
that are loose and easy
and swollen, one blue hair
from my beard, there
by the tiny forest
of almost invisible down.

Aaah . . . aaah . . . .

The sun will wake her.

Seven. Seven blue hairs
on her white garment
of skin. My hair
but not mine now, hers,
her ornament.

My mouth aches.
Inside me is an emptiness
and light pours into it
like ocean into a wrecked ship.

Aaah . . . aaah . . . .

         I think I have not touched her.
         The seven hairs lie there
         but when she wakes
         she will stand and each one will drop
         or the wind catch it, or her fingers
         brush them away, or water
         when she bathes.
                         I have seen
         only her skin, not the nakedness
         beneath, the dark matrix
         of blood and soul.

         When she wakes, her eyes
         will be strange to me.

         Aaah . . . aaah . . . .

9

WIFE: At first, the confusion
      of sleep and waking
      so that I thought
      my marriage was a dream too
      that I would wake from it
      from the sweating tangle
      into a real valley
      of continuous falling.

      Then the face appeared,
      the mask of the dark man.

      This time when he came
      I did not run from him.
      I stood and met his eyes
      and without speaking
      I demanded his secret,

    and as I stared at him
    the features of his face
    melted and altered
    into the known face
    of my husband.   I was afraid
    and not afraid
    and as he reached
    toward me, I turned away
    and was in a forest
    that was at once darkness,
    silence and the vertical
    repetition of the trees.

Then I came out of the forest,
it fell away behind me
and I turned, and the world now
was endless fields of space;
the sky came down in rain
that washed me until
my body seemed all air.
Then grass began to grow
from my skin, and I could not
see myself, for I was not there
or anywhere.   Now I am dreaming
backward into this.

10

WIFE: He is leaving. I cannot
      remember anything.
      I think my childhood
      is the only thing
      I know. I hate
      my childhood.

BLUEBEARD: I do not have the words
 to tell her. It would take
 all my life even to begin
 and I would get it wrong.
 I can only say simply
 do this, not this.

WIFE: Now I cannot see
 his face. I try
 to remember features,
 eyes, mouth, but
 there is only memory
 of past dreams.

BLUEBEARD: Why do I try to speak?
 Words cannot make or unmake
 what must be. Throw down
 the keys. Do not look.
 If I see even the little
 line at the end of her lips
 I will cry out and words
 will imprison me. I hold
 silence in the tight grip
 of both hands. Has all this
 happened before?

11

VOICES: He has an eye in his navel.

 The toes of his feet are webbed.

 He has eaten living things.

 His wives are turned to stone.

 His body is covered with scales.

 The touch of his hand can burn.

He has no sexual organs.

These things have not been seen.
These things are true
because we have all said them.

12

BLUEBEARD: Moving, losing, consider
the random events
at the edge of whatever was,
sunlight, the sound
of water,
      a song
that I once knew.
Meaning nothing and so
everything. Random
happenings, youth, sunlight.

The story is somewhere
else, ahead of me,
but here too

at the edges, seen
out of the corner of the eye.

13

WIFE: The key shines coldly
in sunlight.
Warms in the hand.

It is smithed of hard
iron, and with this
in my hand, I hold
a power.

The indentations of a key
meet metal and decode
resistance. As a cipher
unlocks nonsense,
the key asks and answers.

The force of its
turning will make
time spin forward.

14

BLUEBEARD: I no longer know
if I am travelling
or only waiting.

Sometimes I think all this
is only a story, and every step
is prepared, yet I never know
what the end will be.

Yesterday they showed me
the rack where the skull is stretched
until the mouth must open,
and after the teeth are torn out,
pain becomes a great cave in the head
where words can be inserted.
Then the bodies are broken
into the shape of birds
to sit by the tables of the great
and repeat their devotions.

Once there was a city
built of bones.
I knew I had seen it before
but I could not find my way
for my left and right eye
had been reversed
and I saw in double inversion
and time ran backward.

Sometimes the message tells me
that today I will meet
a man I killed and must
put his soul and body
back together, grip the elastic
spirit and wrap it round
the bones and clasping it with hands
and feet and teeth, throw him down
and breathe in his mouth, force him
to live, his lungs to spread like
   wrinkled paper,
the air make its way into the blood.

And sometimes I wake in the night
when the darkness catches in my throat
and my eyes are useless
and I wonder if this is all a story
that I have told myself, and I go back
to the beginning to tell it again
differently, but I can't remember
clearly enough and I doze and wake
in daylight
        and forget nothing.

15

WIFE: This is only a door.
This one key
is like the others.
Why must I not
open this door?

A secret is knowledge
that we do not know
we do not know.

This room is a part of me
that I have not seen.
I am not myself
until I enter it.

I must enter all
of myself, endure
what I must know,
fill my emptiness
with my emptiness.

16

VOICES: The story must not go on.
It ends here for this is the end.
There are things that do not happen.
and our stories do not tell them.

The words we do not speak
can never make a sound.
The voice the story makes
can only tell itself.

We are the voice of truth
and make the truth we are.
If this were not the end
the end might never come.

WIFE: Now all the doors are lost.
There are no separations.
There is no barrier
between my eyes and ears,
and this garbage of bodies
enters my head
as a worm of noise that
burrows in the ear
and eats the brain.

I am no longer a woman.
For safety, all my atoms
are shared with the stars
and the whale children.

I become the dead women
that I see.
   I cannot want
to leave or look away
from the carnal wreckage.

This is what he wanted
me to discover, or he would
have taken the key.
He wanted me to see this
to know him.
    I will never
tell him.
    Yet he may
know it in some delicacy,
some corruption and easiness
in my touch.
    He will
hold my body and feel
how it is slippery with blood.
Or not.
   I will never
tell him that I know
this much of him.

BLUEBEARD: To come back is a long slide
downhill or the moment at the edge
of sleep when the world falls away.

To come back is to feel the end
of the story is almost on the tongue,
that the words are easy, familiar,
a formula for resolution.

To come back is to be free
of the need to remember
for each detail of the lost face
will soon be held in the eyes.
Presence succeeds absence, time
lies still at the feet.

This is good and familiar, the road,
the smell of fields.

                    Why is my hand
shaking?

        To come back
is loving and easy and dark as sleep.

I have come like this before. My hands
have their own reasons. They
are shaking.

            To come back
is comfort.

         I think of a key.
A word speaks itself. I run
to outrun my fears, but the images
of this return are too familiar.

I know now all that will come.

19

VOICES: The eyes are broken.
        The beard is blue.

        The face is the darkest
        red, almost black;
        there is something
        dies in the colour.

        The head is bare
        wrinkled like earth.

        The eyes are broken
        and the bone caves
        fill with the dry
        and seamed layers of skin.

        The face is gone.
        It is only flesh.
        The eyes are broken.

20

BLUEBEARD: Death is at the edge
        of all life. Death
        is the best name of silence.
        Death is the end
        the true body seeks.

WIFE: I am afraid and not
      afraid. His hands
      are familiar, soft.
      The end is always
      impossible. Now
      I will know everything.

BLUEBEARD: Her breasts lift
  as her arms rise.
  If I am not strong
  and sudden, my hands
  will shape themselves
  into a caress.

WIFE: Now at last
  I can remember the night
  we shared. I feared
  wounding and found
  my body stretched
  like wings unfolding
  from a spine of light.

BLUEBEARD: Always at this moment
  when my hands or knife
  drop towards flesh,
  I no longer believe
  that death is possible.

21

WIFE: My brothers come quickly in
  with the routine elegant gestures
  of challenge and defiance.

  Their teeth shine.
  The eyes of each reflect
  the virile grace of the other.

  They challenge and kill
  with a clean line of movement.
  They tell me
  that I have been rescued

and I ask them who
has been rescued, and they move
toward the door, muttering,
their eyes sullen.

On the floor the head
of my husband lies on one ear,
eyes open watching me.

I lie beside it
and the lips reach out
to kiss me, fail and slacken
and the eyes close.

Somewhere a story
is beginning to happen.

Copyright © 1972 by David Helwig
All rights reserved: no part of this book may be reproduced in any form or by any means, electronic or mechanical, except by a reviewer, who may quote brief passages in a review to be printed in a newspaper or magazine or broadcast on radio or television
Some of these poems have appeared in *Adam*, *Black Moss*, CBC *Anthology*, *Ellipse*, *The Far Point*, *Fiddlehead*, *Galliard*, *Maclean's*, *Quarry*, *Queen's Quarterly*, *Saturday Night*, *Tamarack Review*, *Tribune* (London), *Best Poems of 1968* (Pacific Books), *Best Poems of 1970* (Pacific Books), *How Do I Love Thee* (Hurtig), *Made in Canada* (Oberon), *Rhymes and Reasons* (Holt, Rinehart & Winston), *Storm Warning* (McClelland & Stewart)
Library of Congress Catalogue Card No. 72-77034
ISBN 0 88750 063 3 (hardcover)
ISBN 0 88750 064 1 (softcover)
Cover by Kim Ondaatje. Book design by Michael Macklem
Printed in England by Hazell Watson & Viney Ltd.
PUBLISHED IN CANADA BY OBERON PRESS